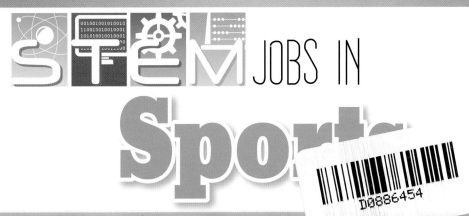

STEM JOBS IN
Sports

Rick Raymos

rourkeeducationalmedia.com

Scan for Related Titles and Teacher Resources

Before Reading:

Building Academic Vocabulary and Background Knowledge

Before reading a book, it is important to tap into what your child or students already know about the topic. This will help them develop their vocabulary, increase their reading comprehension, and make connections across the curriculum.

1. Look at the cover of the book. What will this book be about?
2. What do you already know about the topic?
3. Let's study the Table of Contents. What will you learn about in the book's chapters?
4. What would you like to learn about this topic? Do you think you might learn about it from this book? Why or why not?
5. Use a reading journal to write about your knowledge of this topic. Record what you already know about the topic and what you hope to learn about the topic.
6. Read the book.
7. In your reading journal, record what you learned about the topic and your response to the book.
8. After reading the book complete the activities below.

Content Area Vocabulary
Read the list. What do these words mean?

analyze
artificial
broadcast
calories
composites
concussion
consciousness
durability
obsolete
recovery
specialized
supplements

After Reading:

Comprehension and Extension Activity

After reading the book, work on the following questions with your child or students in order to check their level of reading comprehension and content mastery.

1. Describe the role of STEM in the sports industry. (Summarize)
2. What are some reasons engineers might make improvements to safety equipment? (Infer)
3. What special sports equipment or gear have you used? (Text to self connection)
4. What skills does a team physician need? (Summarize)
5. What developments in sports have made it easier for fans to keep track of the action on the field? (Visualize)

Extension Activity

Create a Venn diagram comparing and contrasting a team physician and a sports dietitian. How are the jobs similar? How are they different?

Table of Contents

What Is STEM?

A nutritionist recommends a **specialized** diet for an Olympic athlete. An engineer tests different materials to use in a new football helmet. An electronics specialist designs a hockey puck that is easier to see on television.

What do all these people have in common? It's not just sports! All their jobs require a STEM education. STEM is a shortcut for talking about science, technology, engineering, and mathematics.

Some of the most exciting careers are in STEM fields. A strong STEM education will allow you to research, test, and build new things. The problem-solving skills learned through STEM can take you to the next level in just about any career field. Find out more about the great STEM jobs that are waiting for you!

Science knowledge is essential when caring for injuries.

What does STEM stand for?

Science
Technology
Engineering
Mathematics

Stats in Sports

For some sports lovers, knowing everything about RBIs, point conversions, and player trades is just part of being a fan. But for others, it can be a full-time job.

Sports statisticians use data from games to show how well the teams and players are performing. They track the details of each and every play.

Every player's stats are updated live during the game.

In baseball, for example, when a player gets a hit, a sports statistician will want to know: what pitch was thrown, how many throws had the pitcher made, how long has the pitcher been playing, when was the last game he pitched, how many at bats did the batter have, where did he hit the ball, what base did he make it to, and who else was on base. And the list goes on. All this data helps statisticians **analyze** the game.

STEM in Action!

RBI, or runs batted in, is a common statistic used in baseball. It credits the batter with every run scored during his at bat. RBI is calculated using simple addition.

Say a player goes to bat and his RBI for that season is 85. If there is one other player on base and he hits a home run, what will his RBI be when he has reached home plate?

85 + 2 = 87

With two runs scored, his RBI will be 87!

Many teams hire their own statisticians. When the score is close and the clock is running down, the coach can ask the statistician for help. What tactics work against the other team? Should we switch pitchers? The statistician will research past data to help decide the next move.

Real STEM Job:
Sports Statistician

A sports statistician has a whole team of people who analyze the professional and college sports games played each week. They gather data about past performances for pre-game shows. They update stats in real time as the games are going on. They share important stats with sports writers and announcers on major sports networks.

This job requires strong math skills. It also requires excellent sports knowledge. Statisticians need to know sports history, current sports events, and understand the issues around future games. Without a doubt, it is a job for sports fans.

Sports statisticians update stats quickly and accurately while the game is still being played.

Engineering Gear

Any sport runs some risk of injury. That's why athletes wear protective gear under their uniforms. From professional athletes to young beginners, pads, shields, and guards are an essential part of play.

But all this extra gear can weigh an athlete down. Designing gear that protects the body while remaining agile is a problem for sports engineers.

Engineers who design protective sporting gear have to consider the way players move on the field. Shoulder pads have to move to allow quarterbacks to throw. Facemasks cannot block a hockey player's view of the puck.

Because each sport is unique, engineers build special gear with that sport in mind. No sports engineer would give a football helmet to a bicyclist! Instead, they design bike helmets that are aerodynamic, helping the rider gain speed during a race.

STEM in Action!

Can you drop an egg without breaking it? What would you need to protect your egg from breaking from a height of 6 feet (2 meters)?

Using materials around your house, create a container or other device to keep the egg safe during its fall. You might want to add padding or a parachute to slow the egg's fall.

Test your device. Was it a success? What can you do to improve your device?

Sports engineers are always looking for ways to improve sporting gear. The gear needs to be light enough for the players to wear all through the game, but also strong enough to protect them from injury.

For this reason, sports engineers have developed special, lightweight plastics. Engineered plastics are used to make goggles, face shields, facemasks, mouth guards, shin guards, braces, shoulder pads, and helmets.

STEM Fast Fact:

Sports injuries have reduced by 46 percent since engineered plastics started being used in protective gear.

STEM Spotlight: Building a Better Helmet

A hard blow to the head can do more than knock you off your feet. It can cause a brain injury known as a concussion. Thousands of athletes suffer from **concussions** every year, from young players to professional athletes.

That is why sports engineers are improving helmet design. They are studying football videos to see how blows occur. They are testing different materials that can better absorb impact. They use this information to figure out how to better protect athletes from injury. With a better helmet, athletes will be safer and able to play as hard as ever.

Helmets cushion the impact when an athlete takes a blow to the head.

Concussions are three times more common among high school athletes than college level players.

Hi-Tech Equipment

It's not just sports gear that's getting a boost. Virtually every piece of sporting equipment has improved with new materials and design. Whether it's the super lightweight bicycles used in the Tour de France or the enlarged rackets of modern tennis players, new equipment gives athletes an edge.

Much of the new equipment design improves its **durability** and reduces injury to athletes. But the improvements also make the equipment more effective.

Take the modern tennis racket. In the early 1960s, rackets were heavy and made from wood. Their heads were also smaller than today's rackets. Lightweight metals and **composites** make rackets easier to swing. The larger heads give the rackets a bigger "sweet spot." This increases the racket's power and reduces elbow strain. A top player with a wooden racket wouldn't stand a chance against a top player with a modern racket.

STEM Fast Fact:

Aluminum bats were banned in major league baseball because they gave the batters too much power. With more players able to hit the ball out of the park, stadiums would have become **obsolete**.

Wood Racket

Composite Racket

STEM in Action!

Smart design can allow an object to move more easily through the air.

Fold two paper airplanes. One should have a pointed nose and the other should have a blunt nose.

Test each airplane. Say the plane with the pointed nose traveled 18 feet and the blunt-nosed plane flew just 7 feet. How much farther did the pointed-nosed plane go?

18 − 7 = 11

The plane with the pointed nose traveled 11 feet farther!

Now, try designing a paper airplane that can beat your first plane. Fold the paper so that you have a smaller plane. Or use a different kind of paper. Test these planes and record your results. What worked? What didn't?

Artificial Turf

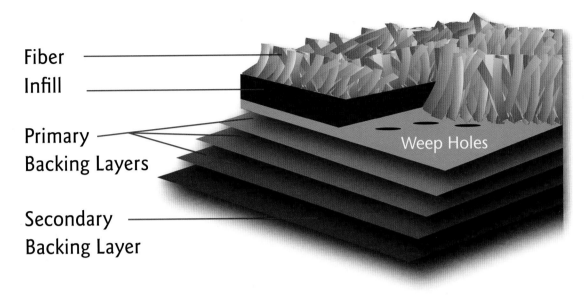

Fiber

Infill

Primary
Backing Layers

Weep Holes

Secondary
Backing Layer

Artificial turf layers are designed to keep the fiber grass in place, provide cushion to those walking on the surface, and allow water to drain.

Sports engineers are also involved in designing the fields, stadiums, and other places where sports are played. Many fields are being converted from grass to **artificial** turf. Turf provides a more even playing field, without dips and divots for athletes to trip on or to slow down the ball. Players can find better footing on turf. They can pivot, turn, and stop more easily. Turf is also designed so that water drains quickly and athletes do not have to play through muddy conditions.

Turf fields have many advantages and have become common in professional, college, and even high school sports. Today, many players prefer turf fields over grass.

Real STEM Job: *Athletic Shoe Designer*

When you go to the store to buy a pair of athletic shoes, you have a wide range of choices. There are shoes for running, walking, and cross training. Some are sport specific for basketball, baseball, football, and soccer. Even more specialized shoes are for wrestling, rock climbing, and cycling. All of these shoes are designed with the athlete in mind.

Companies like Nike, Adidas, New Balance, and Reebok hire athletic shoe designers to create these shoes. The designers need to understand the needs of the athletes and what kind of wear they are going to put on the shoes. They will then prepare blueprints and technical drawings of the shoes, along with the materials to be used.

But creativity is just as important! New designs need to have a great look that will get you to pick those shoes out of all the others in the store.

Sports Medicine

Athletes put their bodies under a lot of stress. Training for long hours helps improve fitness, but also puts athletes at risk of injury. When athletes are injured, they seek advice from doctors who specialize in sports medicine.

Sports injuries often deal with the muscles, ligaments, tendons, or bones. Sports doctors must have a strong knowledge of the muscles and skeleton. They treat sprained ankles, pulled muscles, and other injuries. They also give athletes advice on how they might continue training while recovering from an injury.

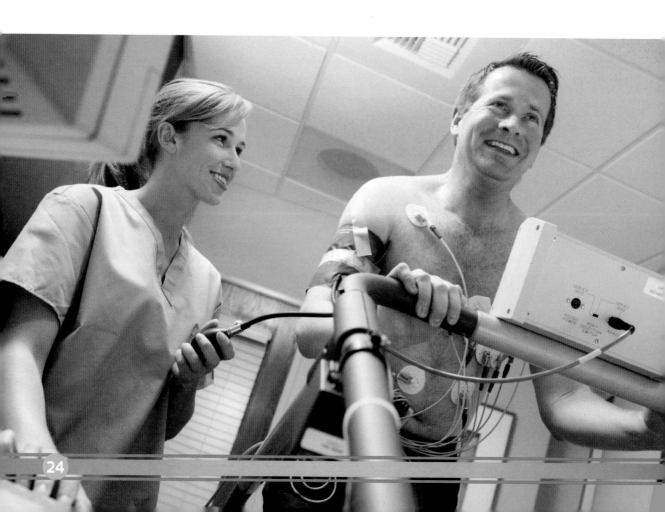

One serious injury that is common in athletes is a concussion. It occurs when the athlete has a sudden blow to the head. This can happen when a player is tackled on a football field or when a rider falls from a bicycle.

Sports doctors check the athletes for signs of confusion or loss of **consciousness**. While many people recover with a few hours of rest, others can suffer serious brain damage. Sports doctors carefully monitor concussions to make sure the athlete is recovering well.

Concussion Injury

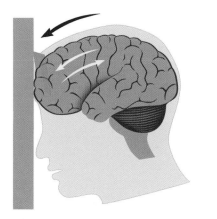 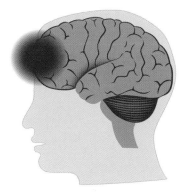

When you receive a hard blow to the head, your brain keeps moving and crashes into your skull.

STEM Fast Fact: Signs of a concussion are headaches, dizziness, blurry vision, and nausea. Concussions are common in such sports as football, boxing, hockey, soccer, skiing, and snowboarding.

STEM in Action!

What effect does exercise have on your body?

While sitting still, find your pulse and count the number of times your heart beats in one minute. Then count how many breaths you take in one minute. Record these numbers.

Now, jog in place for one minute. When you are done, check your pulse again. How did it change? Check your breathing. How did that change?

Try the experiment again after jogging for 5 minutes. Did your pulse and breathing increase? By how much? What would you expect to find after exercising for 10 minutes?

Experts in sports medicine also research exercise. They may want to know how exercise affects people with diabetes. Or they may want to find the best way to build muscle.

They may also research new ways to treat injuries. New medicines and surgeries may improve an athlete's **recovery**. With improved medicine, athletes may be able to return to the field more quickly.

Under the care of a sports doctor, athletes may be able to recover from injuries more quickly.

Real STEM Job:
Team Physician

Most professional teams have one or more team physicians on staff to monitor the players' health. The physicians work directly with the athletes. They are there to treat injuries, prescribe medications, and ensure that players are in good health.

Team physicians will have special knowledge about the kinds of injuries that players are prone to. Physicians for the NFL will know about knee and shoulder tears, concussions, and spinal injuries. But the physicians are trained in all types of medicine. Players can see their team physician about any ailment that is troubling them. The team physician will prescribe the best course of action to get players fully recovered and back on the field.

When an athlete is injured in a game, quick treatment is important.

Fuel for Athletes

After a hard game, your body needs to refuel. You may crave water or a sports drink. Or you may want to chow down on a protein bar.

The right food can help you recover from a hard workout. Sports nutritionists study the body and how it reacts during exercise. They know that during exercise, your body loses a lot of water as well as important nutrients. They recommend drinking water and eating protein to help repair muscles.

Athletes can lose as much as 8 cups (1.9 liters) of water in one hour of intense exercise.

Sports nutritionists are especially important in strength sports, like weight lifting, and in endurance sports, like running or swimming.

For top performance, professional athletes work closely with sports nutritionists. Because nutritionists understand body chemistry, they will recommend special diets based on the workouts. Just because someone is a top athlete does not mean that they are free from illness. Players may need nutritional advice if they have problems with diabetes, high-blood pressure, or food allergies.

STEM Fast Fact:

For healthy living, adults should eat about 2,000 **calories** each day. However, Olympic swimmer Michael Phelps consumed 12,000 calories per day. Phelps needed the extra fuel because he burned so many calories working out.

STEM in Action!

Are you getting your vitamins? A healthy body needs a daily supply of nutrients. But how do you know if you are getting all the nutrients you need?

You can monitor your daily intake of calcium, vitamin C, and iron. You can find the amount of these nutrients that your food contains by checking the Nutrition Facts on food labels.

Keep track of these nutrients all day. Did you meet your daily-recommended value? What nutrients did you not get enough of? Research what foods contain these nutrients.

Continue the experiment! Track your food for the rest of the week and see if you can improve.

Vitamin A 110%	•	Vitamin C 2%
Calcium 10%	•	Iron 3%

*Percent Daily Values are based on a 2,000 calorie diet. Your daily values may be higher or lower depending on your calorie needs.

	Calories	2,000	2,500
Total Fat	Less than	65g	80g
Sat Fat	Less than	20g	25g
Cholesterol	Less than	300mg	300mg
Sodium	Less than	2,400mg	2,400mg
Total Carbohydrate		300g	375g
Dietary Fiber		25g	30g

Calories per gram:

Fat 9	•	Carbohydrate 4	•	Protein 4

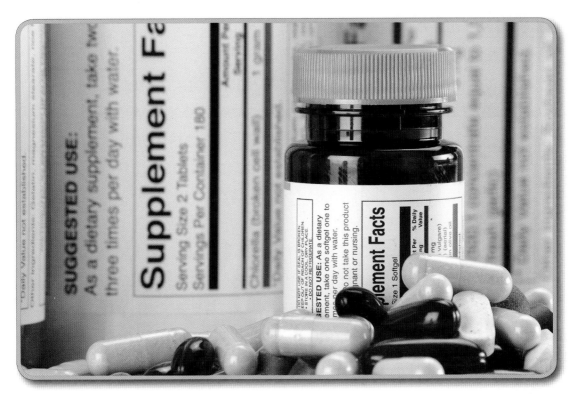

Nutritionists prescribe athletes supplements that are safe and legal. Steroids and other illegal substances may harm an athlete and make them ineligible to compete.

Sometimes, nutritionists will recommend that an athlete take vitamins or other **supplements**. This can be a good way to get nutrients that the athlete is not getting from his or her diet. However, supplements should not replace a balanced diet. The body can better absorb nutrients from real food.

Nutritionists monitor how well athletes perform with their prescribed diet plans. They will make adjustments when the athlete complains of low energy, muscle cramping, or other issues. The nutritionists do their job to keep the athlete's body in top shape.

Real STEM Job:

Sports Dietitian

Dietitians have training in clinical nutrition, dietetics, and biology. They understand body chemistry and know how different nutrients will affect the body. They also understand what impact nutrition can have on disease. This knowledge helps them recommend the right diet for athletes.

Athletes may visit with a sports dietitian to decide what they need to eat. They will describe their training plans and their fitness goals. They will tell the dietitian about any health problems they might have. The dietitian takes this information to design a full meal plan for the athlete.

A sports dietitian may also work with a whole team. The dietitian will give presentations on healthy eating practices. They will recommend various ways that athletes can enhance their performance through diet. They may plan menus for the team and recommend snacks to be eaten prior to, during, or after workouts and competitions.

Broadcasting Sports

When you watch a game on television, you're not just watching the work of the athletes on the field. You're also seeing the hard work of the many people who made that **broadcast** possible.

From tracking the game play to displaying graphics on the field, technology plays a huge role in modern sports broadcasts.

Following the game play is probably the most important part of filming a game. If the camera cannot track the ball, the viewer at home will miss all the action.

Most stadiums and arenas have computer-controlled cameras over the playing area. The cameras move left and right, forward and backward, along suspended cables. These cameras allow viewers at home to get a close-up look at the action on the field.

Behind the scenes, a camera operator uses special software to fly the camera over the field.

STEM in Action!

How would you improve sports on TV?

Watch a game on television. It can be any type of sporting event. Pick something you enjoy to watch.

Do you notice anything that makes the game difficult to watch? Is it hard to keep track of players? To follow the ball?

How would you solve this problem?

It's alright if you don't know how to build the technology that would fix the issue. Just describe something that would improve the game for you. If you study technology, maybe you'll be able to make your idea real one day.

New developments in sports broadcasting have made sports games even easier to watch. If you've watched a professional football game lately, you may have noticed a bright yellow line appear on the field. The line isn't really there. It's computer-generated, and it can only be seen by those watching the game on TV. It marks the line where the next play will start. Before this technology, viewers at home had a hard time knowing how far their team had carried the ball.

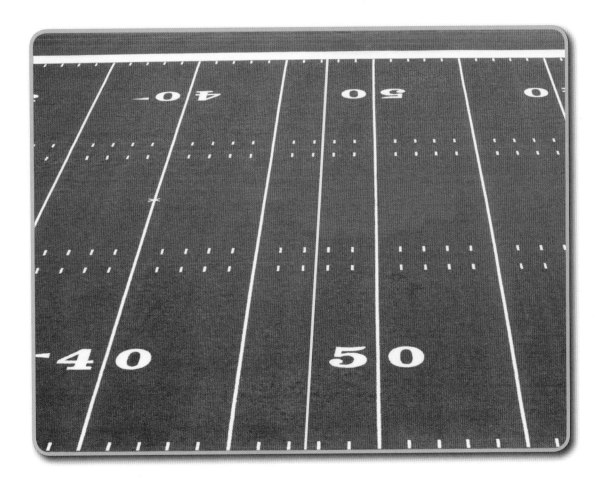

Special features show TV viewers more information than the fans watching the game in the stadium.

Real STEM Job:
Athletic Software Engineer

The technology that made the virtual first and ten lines on football broadcasts possible were made by software engineers. Software engineers have designed systems for football, baseball, soccer, hockey, car racing, and other popular sports. Their technology has also been used when broadcasting the Olympics.

Software engineers look at problems viewers have when watching sports and solutions on how to solve them. They write programs that can track key players and display important statistics. They build technology to track a player's or a ball's path that can be reviewed during a replay. Their work adds to the experience of the viewers at home.

Athletic software engineers write computer programs to make broadcasts more enjoyable.

Advancing Sports with STEM

In the competitive world of sports, athletes are always looking for an edge. This edge may come through advanced training techniques, specialized diet, or hi-tech equipment. For this reason, people with STEM knowledge are essential to the advancement of sports.

By asking questions and searching for solutions, STEM workers can solve problems and improve sports for athletes and fans alike.

STEM Job Fact Sheets

Sports Statistician

Important Skills: Mathematics, Critical Thinking, Science

Important Knowledge: Mathematics, English Language, Computers, Sports

College Major: Mathematics or Statistics

Median Salary: $70,070

Sports Engineer

Important Skills: Complex Problem-Solving, Critical Thinking, Mathematics

Important Knowledge: Engineering and Technology, Design, Mechanics, Mathematics, Physics, Anatomy

College Major: Mechanical or Sports Engineering

Median Salary: $82,480*

*Data provided is for mechanical engineer

Athletic Shoe Designer

Important Skills: Active Listening, Critical Thinking, Speaking, Complex Problem-Solving

Important Knowledge: Design, Engineering and Technology, Production and Processing, Anatomy and Physiology, Computers

College Major: Industrial and Product Design, Packaging Science

Median Salary: $61,890

Team Physician

Important Skills: Speaking, Science, Active Listening, Complex Problem-Solving, Social Perceptiveness

Important Knowledge: Medicine, Biology, Therapy and Counseling

College Major: Medicine, Emergency Medicine, Sports Medicine

Median Salary: $180,870

Sports Dietitian

Important Skills: : Active Listening, Writing, Speaking, Critical Thinking, Reading Comprehension

Important Knowledge: Biology, English, Psychology, Customer Service, Therapy and Counseling

College Major: Clinical Nutrition, Dietetics, Wellness Studies, Biology

Median Salary: $54,370

Software Engineer

Important Skills: Complex Problem-Solving, Programming, Systems Analysis, Systems Evaluation, Judgment and Decision Making

Important Knowledge: Computers and Electronics, Mathematics, English, Engineering and Technology, Customer Service

College Major: Computer Engineering, Computer Programming

Median Salary: $90,410

Glossary

analyze (AN-uh-lize): to examine something carefully to understand it

artificial (ahr-tuh-FISH-uhl): something that is man-made and not found in nature

broadcast (BRAWD-kast): something that is aired on television

calories (KAL-ur-eez): measurement of the amount of energy contained in food

composites (kuhm-PAH-zits): things that are made from multiple materials

concussion (kuhn-KUHSH-uhn): a brain injury that is caused by a hard blow to the head

consciousness (KAHN-shuhs-nis): being aware or awake

durability (door-uh-BIL-i-tee): able to withstand wear and last for a long time

obsolete (ahb-suh-LEET): something that is no longer used; out-of-date

recovery (ri-KUHV-ur-ee): returning to health from illness or injury

specialized (SPESH-uh-lizd): focused on a specific area of study

supplements (SUHP-luh-muhnts): a non-food item that is added to your regular diet

Index

Show What You Know

1. What does STEM stand for?
2. What are some items that engineered plastics have been used to make?
3. How might a team physician help an injured player?
4. Why is it important to eat before exercise?
5. How did the use of composites improve tennis racquets?

Websites to Visit

www.connectamillionminds.com/campaigns/stem-in-sports

www.twcableuntangled.com/2013/06/the-science-of-football-
    racing-and-more-on-stem-in-sports

ionfuture.org

About the Author

Rick Raymos is a writer and sports fan. He plays soccer and watches Mets games at their home field in New York City. Rick has a great fascination with technology and hates to be without his smartphone.

Meet The Author!
www.meetREMauthors.com

www.rourkeeducationalmedia.com

PHOTO CREDITS: Cover © joyt, Steve Debenport, Kriss Russell, CEFutcher; title page © Jim Boardman; page 4, 27 © CEFutcher; page 5 © Gino Santa Maria; page 6 © Cathy Yeulet; page 7 © Karen Foley; page 8 © vladyc; page 9, 10 © Steve Debenport; page 12 © Joe Quinn; page 13 © Andriy Popov, Matt Jacque Photography; page 14 © ayphoto; page 15 © Dave Broberg, JATESADA NATAYO; page 16 © John McAllister; page 17 © skynesher; page 18 © ostill; page 19 © Steve Collender, Yuliyan Velchev; page 20 © Le Do; page 21 © Jen Thomas; page 22 © Nejron Photo; page 23 © Kim Reinick; page 24 © Monkey Business Images; page 25 © alila; page 26 © Levente Gyori; page 28 © Oleksandr Lysenko; page 30 © gchutka; page 31 © BreatheFitness; page 32 © Eugene Feygin; page 33 © monticello; page 34, 35 © stokkete; page 36 © VASILIS VERVERDIS; page 37 © D D; page 38 © mikkelwilliam; page 39 © Danny Hooks; page 40 © Elena Elisseeva; page 43 © asiseeit

Edited by: Jill Sherman

Cover design by: Renee Brady
Interior design by: Jen Thomas

Library of Congress PCN Data

STEM Jobs in Sports / Rick Raymos
(STEM Jobs You'll Love)
ISBN 978-1-62717-696-5 (hard cover)
ISBN 978-1-62717-818-1 (soft cover)
ISBN 978-1-62717-932-4 (e-Book)
Library of Congress Control Number: 2014935490

Printed in the United States of America, North Mankato, Minnesota

Also Available as:

ROURKE'S e-Books